Successful (Happy) Lawyering

Increase Your Bottom Line and Well-Being
One Insight at a Time

By Lee Broekman and Judith Gordon

Foreword by Timothy A. Tosta
Preface by Gilbert A. Holmes

An Actionable Business Journal

E-mail: info@thinkaha.com
20660 Stevens Creek Blvd., Suite 210
Cupertino, CA 95014

Copyright © 2015 Lee Broekman and Judith Gordon

All rights reserved. No part of this book shall be reproduced, stored in a retrieval system, or transmitted by any means electronic, mechanical, photocopying, recording, or otherwise without written permission from the publisher.

Published by THiNKaha®
20660 Stevens Creek Blvd., Suite 210, Cupertino, CA 95014
http://thinkaha.com

First Printing: June 2015
Paperback ISBN: 978-1-61699-143-2   1-61699-143-7
eBook ISBN: 978-1-61699-144-9   1-61699-144-5
Place of Publication: Silicon Valley, California, USA
Paperback Library of Congress Number: 2015932651

Trademarks

All terms mentioned in this book that are known to be trademarks or service marks have been appropriately capitalized. Neither THiNKaha, nor any of its imprints, can attest to the accuracy of this information. Use of a term in this book should not be regarded as affecting the validity of any trademark or service mark.

Warning and Disclaimer

Every effort has been made to make this book as complete and as accurate as possible. The information provided is on an "as is" basis. The author(s), publisher, and their agents assume no responsibility for errors or omissions. Nor do they assume liability or responsibility to any person or entity with respect to any loss or damages arising from the use of information contained herein.

Advance Praise

"*Successful (Happy) Lawyering* reveals over 100 tips to become both a happy and successful lawyer. These precious and insightful nuggets provide a road map for any lawyer to retool and redirect their mode of lawyering and interacting with clients."
Kenneth N. Klee
Professor of Law Emeritus, UCLA School of Law
Partner, Klee, Tuchin, Bogdanoff & Stern LLP

"*Successful (Happy) Lawyering* provides common sense advice that is both thought-provoking and highly useful for improving professional and interpersonal relationships. As an action guide, it will unquestionably be beneficial to any reader who approaches it with an honest, open mind."
Christopher T. Bradford
Partner, Scherer & Bradford

"Judith Gordon and Lee Broekman have created a clear, easy-to-reference guide for lawyers and law students, with innovative, useful insights on each page that will help you create a joyful, fulfilling legal career."
Judi Cohen, Attorney
Founder, WarriorOne: Mindfulness Training for Lawyers
WarriorOne.com

"*Successful (Happy) Lawyering* provides valuable insight and tools that challenge us to adopt a fresh perspective on how we conduct ourselves in order to achieve maximum success and satisfaction in our professional and personal lives."
Amy B. Mallow, Esq.
Career Counselor and Performance Coach, Mallow Consulting Director, Law Firm Management Group, Major, Lindsey & Africa

"A must-read for any attorney looking for quick tools to advance their professional and personal growth. Don't be fooled by its size; every turn of the page in this little book reveals another pearl of wisdom."
Amy Green, CEC, PCC
Dynamic Potential Executive Coaching

"I have worked with Lee for years, and *Successful (Happy) Lawyering* distills many of the lessons she has taught me. This book is necessary reading for any attorney who wishes to be at the top of their game."
Raj Tanden, Shareholder
Buchalter Nemer, PC
Fellow, American College of Tax Counsel

Dedication

To all the lawyers who continue to entrust us with their confidences and allow us to guide them as they build successful, happy careers. Thank you for being our teachers.

Acknowledgments

With gratitude to Jeremy Broekman for his talent, insight and support.

Why We Wrote This Book

Is there a secret to being a happy, successful lawyer? If there is, it is this:
- Be who you are and align your values with your practice, and
- Make all of your relationships—with in-house counsel, outside counsel, opposing counsel, colleagues, peers, management, and subordinates—authentic.

This is easier said than done in a competitive legal environment driven by the bottom line.

Recent studies confirm that when the lives we lead and our core values diverge, well-being plummets. Depression, anxiety, and substance abuse among lawyers has skyrocketed, far outpacing the general population, and attrition from practice is commonplace.

The road to legal-career success is filled with litigating cases, negotiating deals, achieving recognition and acquiring status symbols along the way. It's also a road paved with long hours, high stress, constant conflict, addiction – and depression.

We wrote this guide to invite practicing and aspiring attorneys to take a close look at their personal definitions of success. If you want to achieve health and happiness in your profession, read on.

How do we achieve success and balance in both our professional and personal lives? How do we reap the rewards of a successful law practice without developing unhealthy habits and hurting personal relationships along the way?

To "have it all"—a profitable career and a great life—we need practices that support both. This book presents 140 insights with recent brain science and "how-to" steps for achieving joy and satisfaction in law and in life, in a bite-sized, bottom-line format that is easy for the busy attorney to immediately put to good use.

Keep this guide with you and open it to any section when you need a break or inspiration. Allow the insights you read to put you into the mindset you need to perform at your best.

We have the privilege of coaching and training attorneys at all stages of their careers. We've helped lawyers develop successful legal practices, grow professionally, advance within their firms and flourish in their lives. This guide contains sound bites of the advice we offer to our clients on a daily basis, in the hope that they will help you:

- Make positive, productive choices
- Communicate with confidence and clarity
- Respond to difficult situations proactively
- Enhance your professional and personal interactions
- Achieve your desired results

Thank you for letting us guide you toward successful (happy) lawyering. We invite you to join us in pursuit of loving the law and your life!

Lee Broekman
lee@organiccomm.com
www.linkedin.com/in/leebroekman
www.organiccomm.com
@organiccomm

Judith Gordon
judith@organiccomm.com
www.linkedin.com/in/judithgordon
www.organiccomm.com
@organiccomm

How to Read a THiNKaha® Book
A Note from the Publisher

The THiNKaha series is the CliffsNotes of the 21st century. The value of these books is that they are contextual in nature. Although the actual words won't change, their meaning will change every time you read one as your context will change. Experience your own "aha!" moments ("ahas") with a THiNKaha book; ahas are looked at as "actionable" moments—think of a specific project you're working on, an event, a sales deal, a personal issue, etc. and see how the ahas in this book can inspire your own ahas, something that you can specifically act on. Here's how to read one of these books and have it work for you.

1. Read a THiNKaha book (these slim and handy books should only take about 15-20 minutes of your time!) and write down one to three actionable items you thought of while reading it. Each journal-style THiNKaha book is equipped with space for you to write down your notes and thoughts underneath each aha.
2. Mark your calendar to re-read this book again in 30 days.
3. Repeat step #1 and write down one to three more ahas that grab you this time. I guarantee that they will be different than the first time. BTW: this is also a great time to reflect on the actions taken from the last set of ahas you wrote down.

After reading a THiNKaha book, writing down your ahas, re-reading it, and writing down more ahas, you'll begin to see how these books contextually apply to you. THiNKaha books advocate for continuous, lifelong learning. They will help you transform your ahas into actionable items with tangible results until you no longer have to say "aha!" to these moments—they'll become part of your daily practice as you continue to grow and learn.

As Thought Leader Architect & CEO of THiNKaha, I definitely practice what I preach. I read *#POSITIVITY at WORK tweet*, *#MANAGING YOUR VIRTUAL BOSS tweet*, and one new book once a month and take away two to three different action items from each of them every time. Please e-mail me your ahas today!

Mitchell Levy
publisher@thinkaha.com

Contents

Foreword by Timothy A. Tosta   15

Preface by Gilbert A. Holmes   17

Section I:
On Being Authentic   21

Section II
On Making Conscious Choices   41

Section III
On Being Open-Minded   63

Section IV
On Being Proactive   83

Section V
On Being Innovative   105

Afterword   125

About the Authors   127

Foreword

In this precious little volume, Lee and Judith offer you the opportunity to discover the "art" of lawyering. Everything will change when you discover that the attributes of great lawyers—and leaders—are the attributes of great artists. Among them are authenticity, curiosity, awareness, and creativity, and also by extension, appreciation, effective communication, and above all, nonjudgmental listening.

As a cancer survivor and long-term hospice volunteer, I discovered the artistry of my work from attending well to the particular journey offered by my life. It has been an invaluable discovery! Through their concise, insightful aphorisms, Lee and Judith provide a shortcut on this life-enriching journey of mastery of law and life.

Please enjoy discovering your artistic life of service and prosperity as a lawyer.

Timothy A. Tosta
Partner, Arent Fox

Preface

Lawyers and others in the legal profession often find themselves embroiled in the dueling concepts of success and satisfaction. This significant challenge is not new. In my 40-year career as a practitioner, law professor, and law school dean, one of the constant questions that I have been asked by colleagues and students is, "How can I be both successful and happy as a practicing attorney?" This question sometimes emanates from a conversation that starts with, "I am not happy doing what I'm doing," or, "I am thinking about pursuing another career rather than being a lawyer." With the vast variety of career opportunities that a law degree provides, I have always found it both interesting and worthy of discussion to ask people who are "unhappy" or dissatisfied with their current situation if they are unhappy with the law or unhappy with what they're doing. Most times, the responses have been the latter, which means the question is not whether to leave the law, but if you should leave the particular area where you are practicing or if you should have a different approach to your work and career choices. Satisfaction and success are attainable, but only if you recognize the importance and interdependence of each.

In their book, *Successful (Happy) Lawyering: Increase Your Bottom Line and Well-Being One Insight at a Time*, Lee Broekman and Judith Gordon provide a simple yet powerful step-by-step guide to mastering the interdependence of success and satisfaction. In 1989, I was a successful practitioner in New York City in a practice setting that I started in 1974. I was satisfied, but the edge and the lure of that career seemed to be missing. I then engaged in a process that I called the 3-I: Intentionality (making a decision and acting on it), Innovation (reinventing myself in order to be my best in all areas of life), and Introspection (looking deeply at what mattered most to me and how to make a career out of those things). The result of that process was the decision to enter the legal academy and to do all that was necessary to accomplish that goal. In 1990, I made the transition from the private practice of law to teaching, and have not looked back. Broekman and Gordon offer a comparable approach to living as a successful and satisfied professional

Preface by Gilbert A. Holmes

where the reader can find insight on their current situation or advice on seeking a transition.

Simply put, the intersection of satisfaction and success is the "sweet spot" of life, and this book can help you find it.

Gilbert A. Holmes
Dean
University of La Verne College of Law

Section I: On Being Authentic

Section I
On Being Authentic

This section was born out of a combination of research and personal experience. Perhaps we've all had the experience of feeling like we're one person at the office, and another at home. Many lawyers feel that they have to wear a coat of armor, adopt a certain persona, or be uber competitive in order to establish their authority and gain respect for their work, while reserving being creative, gregarious, empathic, or charitable, for when they're elsewhere.

This disconnect inhibits work satisfaction and client development. Surveys reveal that when it comes to hiring counsel, trust and likeability trump competence; competence is presumed. On a level playing field of competent lawyers, general counsel and potential clients hire people they like and trust. To like and trust you, they have to connect with you authentically. This isn't touchy-feely. In 2002, social scientist Daniel Kahneman won the Nobel Prize in economics for proving that people make important financial decisions, emotionally.[1] The emotional experience in-house counsel and potential clients have when interacting with you and your firm matters, especially when it comes to deciding whether to hire you, or hire you again. Research on the human brain substantiates that it's virtually impossible to make a decision without the involvement of the limbic brain—the brain's emotional processor. We know, too, that in the courtroom, establishing a connection with the jurors is paramount as they take their personal feelings about the lawyers and the parties—their emotional experience—into account in their deliberations.

---

1. "Daniel Kahneman – Facts," Nobelprize.org, accessed December 2, 2014, http://www.nobelprize.org/nobel_prizes/economic-sciences/laureates/2002/kahneman-facts.html.

So how are in-house counsel and other potential clients to connect with us authentically if we are living two lives—"lawyer" at the office and someone else in the world? How do we ensure that potential clients are having positive emotional experiences when interacting with us? When we are authentic at work, relationships with colleagues expand and deepen, trust heightens, the work itself becomes more enjoyable, and clients know it.

Perhaps you've heard the saying, "Your friends become your clients and your clients become your friends." Those attorneys know that authentic relationships build successful law practices that are both fulfilling and sustainable over the long term.

1

To be authentic is to be who you are in whatever you do.

_____

_____

_____

2

Who you are extends beyond what is written on the front of your business card.

_____

_____

_____

Section I: On Being Authentic

3

Bring the person you are beyond attorney-at-law to the office, client meetings, court, etc.

_____

_____

_____

4

When you are authentic in your interactions, you build trust, likeability, and turn contacts into meaningful business relationships.

_____

_____

_____

5

Authentic business relationships underpin, sustain, and grow an attorney's book of business.

Section I: On Being Authentic

6

Focusing solely on your role as a lawyer when engaging potential clients or contacts doesn't allow you to connect on a meaningful level.

7

Business flows by nurturing authentic relationships.

8

Who are you when you're not lawyering?
Who were you before you became a lawyer?

_____
_____
_____

9

Your non-work interests—volunteerism, sports, hobbies, family, travel, fun—connect you to what matters most, and are good for business.

_____
_____
_____

Section I: On Being Authentic

10

Legal work is most meaningful when it is connected with your values.

11

Studies confirm that when we are clear about what matters to us most, and we align those values with our work, we live richer lives.

12

When your values and your practice diverge, well-being plummets, and puts you in danger of burnout, depression, or illness.

13

Practicing habitually, without due attention to your personal values, can bring you wealth, respect, even admiration, but not fulfillment.

Section I: On Being Authentic

14

When you get caught up in what (others say) you should do, you lose sight of what you want and who you really are.

_____
_____
_____

15

Are you living your own life or are you living the life expected of you? Are you listening to your own voice or to external noise?

___

16

Identify what matters to you most, then craft a practice and a life that align with your priorities.

___

Section I: On Being Authentic

17

If you believe that you can't align who you are with your high-paying gig and its high billable hours, note that money follows passion.

18

Where is the passion in your practice? Find it and thrive—financially and personally.

19

Check-in: What is your definition of success? What does it include beyond your professional life?

_____
_____
_____

20

Identify your extrinsic values (financial success, image, approval). Are they driving your life?

_____
_____
_____

Section I: On Being Authentic

21

Identify your intrinsic values (community, family, self-development) and cultivate them.

_____

_____

_____

22

If your drivers are primarily extrinsic, are you living your life or someone else's?

_____

_____

_____

23

Tap into your inner drive to thrive. Who—or what—is driving your life?

_____

_____

_____

Section I: On Being Authentic

24

Looking back on your life from the future, what do you want it to look like? Write it down. Read it regularly. Move toward it.

_____
_____
_____

25

When you live your best life, and are true to yourself, you experience well-being and success.

_____

_____

_____

Section I: On Being Authentic

26

You have permission, and a responsibility, to live your truth and not worry about others' judgment.

_____
_____
_____

27

Acknowledging your role in how you came to this present helps you understand your past and empowers you to create a different future.

_____
_____
_____

28

To be authentic, (1) identify your intrinsic values, (2) align your values and your work, and (3) find the passion in your practice.

_____
_____
_____

Section II: On Making Conscious Choices

Section II
On Making Conscious Choices

We exercise our power to choose every moment of every day. How are the choices you're making impacting your practice, your firm, your life? Are you aware of the moment-to-moment decisions you make and how they impact your life? Are you making choices that serve you?

The quality of our careers and our lives is a direct outcome of the choices we've made in the past and are making in the present. This section is interspersed with strong reminders and concrete steps to help lawyers get actively involved in their daily decision-making process.

Our managers can be difficult and unreasonable, but we can choose to be flexible and understanding in response. Clients can be demanding and disparaging, but we can choose to maintain our boundaries and confidence. Colleagues can be competitive and stressed out, but we can choose to be collaborative and peaceful. Subordinates can be complacent and careless, but we can choose to mentor and guide them.

The most important decisions are not which deals to negotiate or which cases to litigate, but are reflected by how we choose to handle ourselves in daily and momentary situations. Once we recognize that our thoughts, words, and actions impact our professional and personal lives, we choose those thoughts, words, and actions consciously and responsibly.

Section II: On Making Conscious Choices

29

You create the world in which you live and work with each choice you make. Your choices precede, then lead you, wherever you go.

_____

_____

_____

30

Too often, we operate on external influences and from past experience.

_____

_____

_____

31

The moment you recognize that your choices create your circumstances, you are free to make choices that serve you.

_____

_____

_____

Section II: On Making Conscious Choices

32

Are you making choices from fear/worry or with courage/confidence? Or are you not choosing at all? Not choosing is also a choice you make.

_____

_____

_____

33

Do you catch yourself saying, "But I have no choice?"

_____

_____

_____

34

It's never too late to make new choices. It is your responsibility to make choices that improve your life.

35

What is your definition of a quality life and personal success? Take some time to examine this honestly. Are you living your dream?

Section II: On Making Conscious Choices

36

Own your choices; this puts you in charge of your life.

_____
_____
_____

37

Check-in: How do you make decisions? How do your choices reflect your values?

_____

_____

_____

38

Know that you can change anything that concerns your thoughts and actions.

_____

_____

_____

Section II: On Making Conscious Choices

39

Need inspiration? BREATHE for INSPIRATION, which literally means to breathe in.

_____

_____

_____

40

Breathe so that you're able to inspire yourself and your clients.

_____

_____

_____

41

Inhaling deeply triggers the brain's relaxation response. When we're relaxed, our minds open and we think clearly.

Section II: On Making Conscious Choices

42

When we think clearly, we make choices that lead to positive outcomes.

_____

_____

_____

43

You don't get a prize for working until 4:00 a.m. or through lunch...you get rewarded for results; rethink how to achieve them.

_____

_____

_____

44

Practicing in a way that leads to high burnout is self-defeating.

45

Happy, healthy lawyers increase the bottom line. The greater care you take of yourself, the greater success you will have.

Section II: On Making Conscious Choices

46

Envision a life that includes breathing deeply, sleeping well, a daily walk, good nutrition, daily meditation, and daily laughter.

_____

_____

_____

47

Only you can take care of yourself. Any choice that reflects self-care is one that serves you, your firm, your clients, and your family.

48

Practice extreme self-care. Your clients and colleagues benefit from your clarity and well-being.

Section II: On Making Conscious Choices

49

Anxiety is contagious. Positivity is contagious too.

50

Do you create drama or are you in search of peace? You're in charge. Which do you choose?

_____

_____

_____

51

Law firms are high-stress environments. To be calm amidst the chaos, before reacting, ask: "What is the result I want?"

_____

_____

_____

52

When you choose to be calm and collected, you are more likely to achieve the results you want, in work and in life.

_____

_____

_____

53

We choose the way in which we interact and communicate, and therefore we also choose whether we will create fulfilling lives for ourselves and others.

54

Is your approach to client development, "What's in this for me?" or "How might I be of service?" Which is more likely to land the client?

Section II: On Making Conscious Choices

55

Law is a service industry. Whose agenda are you serving?

___

___

___

56

Attorneys who foster good client relationships don't get sued when mistakes are made. Good relationships provide room for resolution.

___

___

___

57

Clear communication brings us incredible personal and professional fulfillment.

_____

_____

_____

58

Control is illusory. Do your best and let that lead you. Don't stress over what others say or do. You're only in charge of yourself.

_____

_____

_____

Section II: On Making Conscious Choices

59

Situation + Response = Outcome

You're in charge of how you respond to external events and THAT determines the outcome. What serves you?

60

It's amazing how we get what we want if we just ask for it in a way that people can hear—from a place of mutual respect.

61

To make conscious choices, (1) note moment-to-moment decisions, (2) understand the outcome that serves you best, and (3) choose accordingly.

_____
_____
_____

Section III: On Being Open-Minded

Section III
On Being Open-Minded

As professionals in the area of attorney development, we regularly receive feedback from lawyers who report the magical workings of being open-minded. The power of this simple yet significant mindset is expansive and life-changing.

One corporate attorney we know was astonished to discover that when he brought an open mind instead of his own agenda to a pitch meeting, the prospective client gave him all the information he needed to make his pitch persuasive. He learned to listen to the client's stated needs and wants without preconceptions and assumptions. The client felt heard and the attorney was able to identify and address the client's unmet need.

Another lawyer we know was both happy and relieved that he decided to approach a highly sensitive and stressful discussion with open-mindedness and nonjudgment. A client he brought into the firm was reneging on a contract and defaulting on promised payment. The lawyer had all sorts of views and ideas about why the client was defaulting and how to get him to pay. But since none of these approaches and proposals had previously worked, he consciously chose to open his mind before his mouth, and the results were dramatically different. The client explained his situation and they were able to arrive at a mutually beneficial payment plan.

We can train our minds to be clear and open by being both present and curious. Lawyers are taught to have all of the answers, but this can get in the way of hearing new suggestions and ideas that lead to more powerful possibilities.

Section III: On Being Open-Minded

62

Being open-minded means suspending judgment in your daily practice and replacing it with curiosity.

_____
_____
_____

63

Create the life you want, grow as a human being, and experience success regularly by keeping an open mind.

_____

_____

_____

Section III: On Being Open-Minded

64

When you have an open mind, you attract clients and opportunities. Expand and explore beyond your experience, expertise, and expectations.

_____

_____

_____

65

Progress and growth are achieved when you keep an open mind.

_____

_____

_____

66

To advance your life and work, be willing to experience new things, or experience things differently.

Section III: On Being Open-Minded

67

An open mind is a nonjudgmental mind. Notice how often you're judging other people and situations.

68

We judge people and situations as right/wrong, strong/weak, winners/losers, rich/poor, smart/foolish, constricting our perspective.

_____
_____
_____

Section III: On Being Open-Minded

69

When we make judgments based on either/or and this-or-that, we limit our thinking as attorneys to come up with outstanding outcomes.

70

Judgmental thoughts are binary, only allowing for two options, constricting our ability to be creative, expansive, and imaginative.

71

To open your mind to new solutions, imagine at least four different perspectives to the situation facing you (instead of just two).

_____
_____
_____

72

When we expand to seeing four or more possibilities, we open up to opportunities, and become more creative and successful lawyers.

_____
_____
_____

Section III: On Being Open-Minded

73

Opportunities are presented to us regularly, but we risk missing them when we stay in a limited mindset.

_____
_____
_____

74

To increase the odds for success, recognize opportunities by keeping an open mind.

Section III: On Being Open-Minded

75

To keep an open mind, be present and be curious; actively listen to other points of view.

76

Being present means turning our *entire* attention to the person (client, colleague, judge, etc.) who is speaking.

77

Being curious means that we listen without any preconceived notions about what is being said.

_____

_____

_____

Section III: On Being Open-Minded

78

When we listen to our own thoughts more than to the other person in the conversation, we are not listening effectively.

_____

_____

_____

79

People and circumstances that show up in our lives present us with opportunities to improve, evolve, and advance.

_____

_____

_____

80

An open mindset is receptive to suggestions and ideas. A narrow mind, like a horse with blinders, sees only one path.

81

People avoid or bypass speaking with those who see only one way of doing things and who come off as opinionated and argumentative.

Section III: On Being Open-Minded

82

A dogmatic and hardheaded mindset is unproductive. Life is not black or white. You may be overlooking details and deeper insights.

83

When we limit our worldview, we literally close our mind's capacity to see multiple perspectives and choices.

84

An open mind allows us to address clients' unmet needs.

Section III: On Being Open-Minded

85

To be open-minded, (1) suspend judgment, (2) listen with curiosity (3) consider others' positions—clients, opposing parties, colleagues, etc.

_____

_____

_____

Section IV: On Being Proactive

Section IV
On Being Proactive

A senior partner was telling us that she'd "had it for the last time" with associates making careless mistakes that made the firm look bad to a prestigious client. She believed that she had set all the processes in place to prevent and avoid misspellings of names, inaccurate information regarding ages and titles, and more problematic issues, such as the omission of complete paragraphs from important documents.

Feeling justifiably frustrated and under intense pressure, she was ready to react and reprimand. But then she remembered that she'd done that before—countless times and with unsatisfactory results. Associates still waited until the last minute, believed that they could do it their way, missed directives and deadlines, and angered the client.

So she paused. She took a breath. She took a walk.

This short time and distance allowed the partner to craft the best approach for getting positive results from her associates. Instead of reacting, she asked the associates to design their own accountability plan for meeting deadlines and avoiding recurring mistakes.

By being proactive, she resisted a negative, automatic, habitual, and pointless reaction, and replaced it with a positive, intentional, and effective response.

Our modes of thinking are often limited to conditioned reactive responses. The patterns and habits we've developed over a lifetime cause us to make the same assumptions, form the same conclusions, and make the same decisions. Over and over again.

Automatic, habitual thinking doesn't lead to growth.

The most direct way to improve our communication is to convert our reactive thoughts and beliefs into proactive ones.

Section IV: On Being Proactive

86

Proactive lawyers respond to change and challenges with new strategies and innovative approaches.

_____

_____

_____

87

Lawyer A: "How's it going?"

Lawyer B: "It's going."

Lawyer A: "Is it going in the direction you want?"

Lawyer B: "Huh?"

What's your answer?

_____

_____

_____

Section IV: On Being Proactive

88

Life is growth in a positive direction.

89

Automatic, habitual thinking doesn't lead to growth. An untrained mind is filled with reactive thoughts and limiting beliefs.

90

We train our minds to think proactively by substituting negative reactions with positive, productive responses.

_____
_____
_____

Section IV: On Being Proactive

91

Reacting negatively is deceiving because overpowering another or "controlling" a situation gives us a feeling of false elation.

92

Releasing negative emotions in the form of bitter outbursts, outspoken denunciations, and verbal tirades impede success and happiness.

93

We react when we are disappointed and when things don't go the way we wish.

94

There's a difference between reacting and responding.

Section IV: On Being Proactive

95

Do you RESPOND or REACT?

Before you react: PAUSE.

Let the emotion dissipate.

Respond from a clearer you.

_____

_____

_____

96

External events trigger reactive emotions.
Let your emotions guide you, not rule you.

_____
_____
_____

Section IV: On Being Proactive

97

Make the following agreement: "Each time I am triggered, I will slow my breath and listen; I will not react in word or action."

_____

_____

_____

98

When you respond to an alarm, do you freak out or move calmly toward safety? You have options.

_____

_____

_____

99

To defuse your emotions: BREATHE, walk, read an inspiring quote, watch a funny video, listen to music, drink tea, talk to a friend.

_____

_____

_____

Section IV: On Being Proactive

100

Practice detached involvement. This means that we keep our emotional distance while staying intellectually engaged.

101

When we listen, breathe, and respond calmly, we make a large deposit into our life's satisfaction and success account.

102

We have tens of thousands of thoughts per day. Most of our thoughts are repetitive and most of those thoughts are negative.

Section IV: On Being Proactive

103

Pay attention to your self-talk. What we say to ourselves has a major impact on how we communicate with other people.

_____

_____

_____

104

Ask yourself: "Would I say this aloud to a child in my life?"

_____

_____

_____

105

We choose how we think and speak about ourselves. Self-deprecation is self-defeating.

Section IV: On Being Proactive

106

The most direct way to improve our communication is to convert our reactive thoughts and beliefs into proactive ones.

107

Obstacles are opportunities for growth.

108

If I give you $1M for every challenge you master, you will start seeking out obstacles and embracing them as opportunities to grow richer.

_____

_____

_____

109

Proving that we are right and others are wrong, and calling out others' mistakes in our own defense, is reactive and destructive.

_____

_____

_____

Section IV: On Being Proactive

110

We can't focus on what matters most if our minds are filled with worries, regrets, expectations, and disappointments.

_____

_____

_____

111

Challenging people and situations show up in our lives to provide us with opportunities to practice being proactive.

_____

_____

_____

Section IV: On Being Proactive

112

We're not challenged by people and situations. We're challenged by our (in)ability to listen attentively and communicate proactively.

_____

_____

_____

113

We become powerful when we conquer our reactionary, impulsive urge to lash out or shut down.

_____

_____

_____

114

To be proactive, (1) focus on the desired outcome, (2) take responsibility, and (3) respond with the clarity of emotional distance.

Section V: On Being Innovative

Section V
On Being Innovative

Innovative thinking is essential to successful lawyering. In many facets of the practice, originality, imagination, creativity, and experimentation are required in order to succeed.

As negotiators, legal actors more effectively accomplish their goals when they seek innovative solutions to legal problems and transactions. When multiple parties are involved, the successful lawyer will focus on each of the objectives and creatively satisfy the needs and interests of all. This innovative problem-solving approach maximizes and accelerates the client's gain while winning the lawyer accolades and financial favor.

Life is not linear. Clients and cases are not neat. The lawyer, therefore, must also be an out-of-the-box thinker and actor. When attorneys try on different ways to frame legal problems, they establish the opportunity for original outcomes. Creative, innovating lawyers feel less bound by traditional boilerplate language and thus expand the existing domain of legal resolutions.

There isn't only one way to think like a lawyer. Successful lawyering requires going beyond basic analytic and analogical thinking and increasing our imaginative and creative intelligence.

Section V: On Being Innovative

115

Being innovative means applying curiosity to your legal analysis.

116

New clients, new cases, and new deals all require new thinking.

117

Successful lawyers welcome each new client, new case, and new deal with new thinking.

118

A client-driven legal market requires lawyers to adopt strategies that provide clients with high-quality service.

Section V: On Being Innovative

119

Originality is the foundation of innovative legal thinking.

120

Innovative beliefs are internal.

"I see opportunities where others see problems."

"My self-worth is not dependent upon what others think."

121

Reactive beliefs are external.

"I need to be in control."

"I need to live up to others' standards" (parents, partners, peers).

_____

_____

_____

Section V: On Being Innovative

122

Innovative thinking leads to infinite choices, possibilities, and solutions.

123

Successful attorneys develop innovative alliances and collaborative efforts.

124

When attorneys try on different ways to frame legal problems they establish the opportunity for original outcomes.

Section V: On Being Innovative

125

What do you see: ECVARITE
REACTIVE?
CREATIVE?

_____
_____
_____

126

Reactive thinking depletes the legal mind; creative thinking replenishes it.

_____
_____
_____

127

Creative insights are generated when we proactively try on different perspectives.

_____

_____

_____

Section V: On Being Innovative

128

Attorneys succeed when they overcome their resistance to change by accepting the challenge to adopt new approaches to their practices.

_____
_____
_____

129

Innovative thinking allows lawyers to overcome sluggish productivity and to financially prosper.

Section V: On Being Innovative

130

To be innovative, approach the issue with curiosity ("What don't I know?") and ask open-ended questions ("What's a new approach?").

131

Are there other perspectives to the problem as the client has framed it? Unknown circumstances? Underlying motives? Hidden agendas?

132

What solution does the client seek? What options might you create? What is the desired outcome? What would a "win" look like?

Section V: On Being Innovative

133

Instead of forcing your mind to come up with solutions, allow your thinking to flow in the direction of fulfilling desirable outcomes.

134

The energy of innovative thinking is lighthearted, motivating, invigorating, and empowering—and leads to happy clients.

135

Not using a creative process leads to feeling stuck, exhausted, frustrated, and depleted—and doesn't serve the client.

Section V: On Being Innovative

136

We have participated in creating our present life. And every day, we are creating our future life. Do you like what you're creating?

_____

_____

_____

137

The results of innovative thinking are a million-fold more gratifying, and follow the natural pattern of effortless and painless pursuit.

_____

_____

_____

138

Lawyers are taught to be analytical. Analytical thinking does not preclude creative problem-solving.

Section V: On Being Innovative

139

To be innovative, (1) approach the issue with curiosity, (2) ask open-ended questions, and (3) reframe the issues creatively.

_____
_____
_____

140

To be a successful and happy lawyer, *choose* to be authentic, open-minded, proactive and innovative.

Afterword

While some lawyers appear to achieve success and happiness effortlessly, for most of us, it is an intentional process. By being intentional about what successful (happy) lawyering means to you each day—and owning it—success and happiness, as you define it, is yours.

What Are Your Ahas?

Thanks for reading *Successful (Happy) Lawyering*!

Got any "Ahas" that would fit with this book?

We'd love for you to share them!

Tweet us **@thinkaha** and/or **@organiccomm**, and tag your Ahas with **#successfulhappylawyering**.

About the Authors

Lee Broekman, MA, principal of Organic Communication, provides communication and management guidance to law firms. A professor and coach, Lee is an expert in persuasion, presentation, and interpersonal communication. A frequent speaker in legal gatherings, Lee trains AmLaw 100 law firm leaders. She shows attorneys how to attract clients, increase firm productivity, innovate legal service, and adopt smart strategies.

Judith Gordon, Esq., principal of Organic Communication, provides communication, leadership, and professional development direction to law firms and their lawyers, helping them develop business, increase visibility, enhance their reputations, and lead more productive, satisfying lives. Judith teaches at UCLA School of Law, is a certified mediator and coach with expertise in social and emotional intelligence.

Books in the THiNKaha® Series

The THiNKaha book series is for thinking adults who lack the time or desire to read long books, but want to improve themselves with knowledge of the most up-to-date subjects. THiNKaha is a leader in timely, cutting-edge books and mobile applications from relevant experts that provide valuable information in a fun, Twitter-brief format for a fast-paced world.

They are available online at http://thinkaha.com or at other online and physical bookstores.

1. *#AFTER COLLEGE tweet* by Matthew Chow and Jonathan Chu
2. *#B2B STRATEGIC PRICING tweet* by Bob Bonacorsi, CPP
3. *#BOOK TITLE tweet* by Roger C. Parker
4. *#BUSINESS SAVVY PM tweet* by Cinda Voegtli
5. *#COACHING tweet* by Sterling Lanier
6. *Coffee Crazy* by Robert Galinsky
7. *#CONTENT MARKETING tweet* by Ambal Balakrishnan
8. *#CORPORATE CULTURE tweet* by S. Chris Edmonds
9. *#CORPORATE GOVERNANCE tweet* by Brad Beckstead, CPA, CISA, CRISC
10. *#CREATING THOUGHT LEADERS tweet* by Mitchell Levy
11. *#CROWDSOURCING tweet* by Kiruba Shankar and Mitchell Levy
12. *#CULTURAL TRANSFORMATION tweet* by Melissa Lamson
13. *#DEATHtweet Book01: A Well-Lived Life through 140 Perspectives on Death and Its Teachings* by Timothy Tosta
14. *#DEATH tweet Book02: 140 Perspectives on Being a Supportive Witness to the End of Life* by Timothy Tosta
15. *#DEMAND GENERATION tweet* by Gaurav Kumar
16. *#DIVERSITYtweet* by Deepika Bajaj
17. *#DOG tweet* by Timothy Tosta and Nancy Martin
18. *#DREAMtweet* by Joe Heuer
19. *#ENDURANCE tweet* by Jarie Bolander
20. *#ENGAGE tweet* by Maryann Baumgarten, PhD, and Lisa Smith
21. *#ENTRYLEVELtweet Book01: Taking Your Career from Classroom to Cubicle* by Heather R. Huhman
22. *#ENTRY LEVEL tweet Book02: Relevant Advice for Students and New Graduates in the Day of Social Media* by Christine Ruff and Lori Ruff

23. *#EXPERT EXCEL PROJECTS tweet* by Larry Moseley
24. *#GOOGLE+ for BUSINESS tweet* by Janet Fouts
25. *#GREAT BOSSES tweet* by S. Chris Edmonds, MHROD
26. *#HEALTHCARE REFORM tweet* by Jason T. Andrew
27. *#IT OPERATIONS MANAGEMENT tweet* by Peter Spielvogel, Jon Haworth, Sonja Hickey
28. *#JOBSEARCHtweet* by Barbara Safani
29. *#LEADERSHIPtweet* by Kevin Eikenberry
30. *#LEADS to SALES tweet* by Jim McAvoy
31. *#LEAN SIX SIGMA tweet* by Dr. Shree R. Nanguneri
32. *#LEAN STARTUP tweet* by Seymour Duncker
33. *#MANAGING UP tweet* by Tony Deblauwe and Patrick Reilly
34. *#MANAGING YOUR VIRTUAL BOSS tweet* by Carmela Southers
35. *#MILLENNIALtweet* by Alexandra Levit
36. *#MOJOtweet* by Marshall Goldsmith
37. *#MOVING OUT tweet* by Gabrielle Jasinski, Eliza Lamson, Elizabeth Wassmann, and Hannah Miller
38. *#MY BRAND tweet* by Laura Lowell
39. *#OPEN TEXTBOOK tweet* by Sharyn Fitzpatrick
40. *#PARTNER tweet* by Chaitra Vedullapalli
41. *#PLAN to WIN tweet* by Ron Snyder and Eric Doner
42. *#POSITIVITY at WORK tweet* by S. Chris Edmonds, MHROD and Lisa Zigarmi, MAPP
43. *#POWER KIDS tweet* by Rudy Mui and Shirley Woo
44. *#PRESENTATION tweet* by Wayne Turmel
45. *#PRIVACY tweet* by Lori Ruff
46. *#PROJECT MANAGEMENT tweet* by Guy Ralfe and Himanshu Jhamb
47. *#QUALITYtweet* by Tanmay Vora
48. *#RISK MANAGEMENT tweet* by Cinda Voegtli & Laura Erkeneff
49. *#SCRAPPY GENERAL MANAGEMENT tweet* by Michael Horton
50. *#SCRUM tweet* by Utpal Vaishnav
51. *#SKATEBOARDING tweet* by Tad Malone
52. *#SOCIAL MEDIA PR tweet* by Janet Fouts
53. *#SOCIALMEDIA NONPROFIT tweet* by Janet Fouts with Beth Kanter
54. *#SPORTS tweet* by Ronnie Lott with Keith Potter
55. *#STANDARDS tweet* by Karen Bartleson

56. *#STUDENT SUCCESS tweet* by Marie B. Highby and Julia C. Schmitt
57. *#SUCCESSFUL CORPORATE LEARNING tweet Book01: Profitable Training by Optimizing your Customer and Partner Education Organization* by Terry Lydon and Mitchell Levy
58. *#SUCCESSFUL CORPORATE LEARNING tweet Book02: Critical Skills All Learning Professionals Can Put to Use Today* by Bill Cushard and Mitchell Levy
59. *#SUCCESSFUL CORPORATE LEARNING tweet Book03: Instructional Design for Today's Professionals* by Vicki Halsey, S. Chris Edmonds, and Mitchell Levy
60. *#SUCCESSFUL CORPORATE LEARNING tweet Book04: Career Transition Training and Services That Work in Today's Environment* by Barbara Safani and Mitchell Levy
61. *#SUCCESSFUL CORPORATE LEARNING tweet Book05: Everything You Need to Know about Knowledge Management in Practice in 140 Characters or Less* by Michael Prevou and Mitchell Levy
62. *#SUCCESSFUL CORPORATE LEARNING tweet Book06: Creating a Learning Culture with 140 Specific Ideas for Building Continual Learning into Organizational Life* by Kevin Eikenberry and Mitchell Levy
63. *#SUCCESSFUL CORPORATE LEARNING tweet Book07: Everything You Need to Know about Communities of Practice* by Mike Hower, Michael Prevou, and Mitchell Levy
64. *#SUCCESSFUL CORPORATE LEARNING tweet Book08: 140 Tips and Tricks for Creating and Delivering Powerful, High-Quality Webinars, and Virtual Learning Events* by Sharyn Fitzpatrick and Mitchell Levy
65. *#SUCCESSFUL CORPORATE LEARNING tweet Book09: Collaborative Tools and Techniques to Empower Productivity and Learning* by David Coleman and Mitchell Levy
66. *#SUCCESSFUL CORPORATE LEARNING tweet Book10: Making Learning Stick—Transforming Knowledge into Performance* by John Moxley, PhD, and Mitchell Levy
67. *#TEAMWORK tweet* by Caroline G. Nicholl
68. *#THINKtweet* by Rajesh Setty
69. *#THOUGHT LEADERSHIP tweet* by Liz Alexander, PhD and Craig Badings
70. *#TOXINS tweet* by Laurel J. Standley, PhD
71. *Jill Rowley on #SocialSelling* by Jill Rowley
72. *Ted Rubin on ROR #RonR* by Ted Rubin
73. *The Unofficial Harry Potter Spell Book* by Duncan Levy
74. *The Unofficial Whovian Rule Book* by Duncan Levy

www.ingramcontent.com/pod-product-compliance
Ingram Content Group UK Ltd.
Pitfield, Milton Keynes, MK11 3LW, UK
UKHW021303180426
11947UKWH00015B/991